Joy Thoughts!
Joy Truths!

Joy Thoughts! Joy Truths!

Ruth J. Scott

XULON PRESS

Xulon Press
2301 Lucien Way #415
Maitland, FL 32751
407.339.4217
www.xulonpress.com

© 2021 by Ruth J. Scott

All rights reserved solely by the author. The author guarantees all contents are original and do not infringe upon the legal rights of any other person or work. No part of this book may be reproduced in any form without the permission of the author.

Due to the changing nature of the Internet, if there are any web addresses, links, or URLs included in this manuscript, these may have been altered and may no longer be accessible. The views and opinions shared in this book belong solely to the author and do not necessarily reflect those of the publisher. The publisher therefore disclaims responsibility for the views or opinions expressed within the work.

Unless otherwise indicated, Scripture quotations taken from the New King James Version (NKJV). Copyright © 1982 by Thomas Nelson, Inc. Used by permission. All rights reserved.

Paperback ISBN-13: 978-1-66283-242-0

Dedication

This book is dedicated:
to my sons, Darrell, Reginald, Timothy, Phillipp
to my daughters, Anita, Kendra, Reba, Christine
to my daughters-in-love, Mackenzie, Christian, Preeti, Saundra
to my son-in-love, Caleb
to my sister, Cynthia
to my husband, James
to my friend, Kimberly, who insisted that I obey the Lord and continue working on this book.
To my friend, Margo, who believes that God has something special for me.
To my friends and prayer partners, Sheila, Margo, Shirley and Patti.
Special thanks to my daughter Kendra, daughters-in-love, Christian, Preeti and Mackenzie for proofreading and critiquing the manuscript.
So grateful to Christian and my sister Cynthia for helping me with submitting my manuscript.
Much appreciation to Cari and the entire support team for helping my dream for this book to come to fruition.

Bio

A proud and loving wife, mother, grandmother and great grandmother, Ruth is a Christian, an American and unapologetically frequently a couch potato. She is a prayer warrior and intercessor and on occasions, she coordinates and teaches Bible group studies. She likes her "alone time" with the Lord. Her favorite past time is reading and studying the Word of God. Spending time with the grands, attending family gatherings and outings and fellowshipping with close knit friends brings her great pleasure.

When you read *Joy Thoughts! Joy Truths!* Ruth hopes you will experience the presence of the Lord and the Joy that He offers.

These Joy Thoughts and Joy Truths are brief yet pithy meditations and sayings that are simple but something to think about truths. Though the are short, these joy messages remind us to "rejoice always" to "be cheerful", to "be merry" to "arise and shine" and to just enjoy the Goodness and the Presence of God.

The Joy Thoughts and Joy Truths are really just utterances of our close encounters with God. These sayings encourage us to welcome and embrace Joy during the good times and the not-so-good times. These Joy Thoughts and Joy Truths help us to realize that the spirit of Joy is real.

Make a Joyful shout to the Lord,
all you lands!
Serve the Lord with gladness;
Come before His Presence with singing.
(Psalm 100:1-2) NKJV

Now may the God of hope fill you
with all Joy and peace
in believing, that you may
abound in hope by the power of
the Holy Spirit.
(Romans 15:13) NKJV

Joy Thoughts! Joy Truths!

Joy is a cheerful salutation
that begins your morning and
brightens your whole day.

Description of Joy:
Sunny and bright.

Joy Thoughts! Joy Truths!

Joy is beginning your day
with the Son.

Your Joy speaks to the heart of God.

Joy is that tattletale sign
that God is present.

No matter what you put on,
Nothing, absolutely nothing looks
better on you than the garment of
Joy.

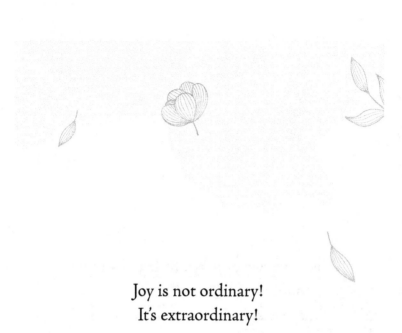

Joy is not ordinary!
It's extraordinary!

You have two opportunities to be Joyful.
Number 1: When all is going well.
Number 2: When all is not going well.

Joy: Optimism released
and
Unleashed optimism

The Joy Cycle
When you have Joy, you give Joy. When
you give Joy you get Joy. When you get Joy you
give Joy. When you give Joy you have
Joy.

Feeling somewhat down in the dumps? Let Joy lift you up.

Joy is right here on earth
just as it is in Heaven.

Joy is the fruit of
great expectations.

Joy, unlike flattery, is the real deal.

Joy always comes in the morning
bringing in the Son.

Joy is never at the expense of another person's misfortune.

A day without Joy is a weak day.

Joy is not a hidden treasure.
It is an opened present.

Joy Thoughts! Joy Truths!

Joy! That healing balm for
whatever ails you.

Abundant Joy refreshes your whole being: spirit, soul, mind and body.

Joy is Jesus loving you so much
that He doesn't want to live
without you.

Joyful is not just a state of mind
but a state of being.

Joy is absolutely essential for
a blessed and fulfilling life.

If you never experience Joy here on
earth you definitely will feel
out of place in Heaven.

Joy is a perfect pain killer
with no side effects.

Joy is the greatest weapon against stress and anxiety, lies and deceit, disrespect and disobedience, lack and poverty, criticism and insults, sickness and diseases, destruction and despair and any and all assaults of the enemy.

Joy is never ever passive, but
it is forever and always passionate.

Joy Full vs. Joy Less!
No contest.
Joyful always wins over joyless.

The spirit of Joy drives out
the spirit of heaviness.

Joy is not a fact. Facts change.
Joy is truth. It never changes.

Joy, like life, is eternal.

Joy is like the Duracell Bunny.
It just keeps on going and going.

Suffering exists
But
Praise the Lord!
So
Does Joy.

You really should let Joy be your daily habit.

Joy is the Son rising up in you.

Joy is giving God praise as
only you can!

Don't settle for being good and happy when you can be well and Joyful.

Joy ushers you into God's Presence.

Joy is basking in the Son all
day and not getting sunburned.

Joy energizes you to face
"Whatever!"

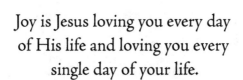

Joy is Jesus loving you every day of His life and loving you every single day of your life.

Instead of being full of yourself, be full of Joy.

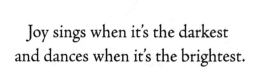

Joy sings when it's the darkest
and dances when it's the brightest.

Joy has both participants and spectators.

Whatever the problem is, Joy
and chocolate can fix it.

Joyful people shine, nourish,
rejoice, and serve with gladness.

Looking for Joy? Just look around.
It's right there.

Joyful people don't just survive.
They thrive.

Joy has no off days.

Joy is as old as Creation;
Yet it never grows old.

Joy really is a good addiction.

Joy and boredom!
There's no comparison!

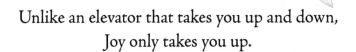

Unlike an elevator that takes you up and down,
Joy only takes you up.

Joy is the oil of gladness.

He who has Joy has abundant life.

Want some Joy? Then be a cheerful giver.

Joy doesn't let you down.
It lifts you up.

It's not lucky to have Joy. It's a blessing.

It's hard to be thankful and not be joyful.
Likewise, it's hard to be joyful and not
be thankful.

If you settle for being happy you
may never experience Joy.

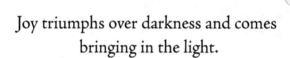

Joy triumphs over darkness and comes bringing in the light.

Be a contributor and not just a consumer of Joy.

Joy can't change your past, but it can help you to let it go, and move on in victory and delight.

It is imperative for Joy to dwell in a vessel of praise. May you be such a vessel.

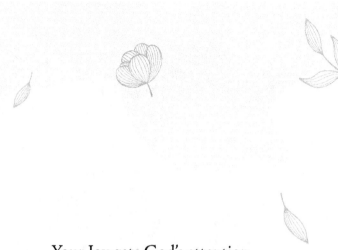

Your Joy gets God's attention.

Joy is not entitlement. It's enlightment.

A person with Joy is a person
with a good attitude.

Joy is a hug and kiss from
God the Father.

Joy annoys the joyless.

Joy is fantastic not fantasy.

Joy translation: God is good!

Joy has limited vision. It only looks upward.

Joy is fluent and articulate in any language.

Joy is not a task, duty or chore.
It's a gift.

Joy doesn't need a time out.

When you think Joy, you don't
think gloom and doom.

Joy has no expiration date.

Joy is the best picker upper
for a downcast and contrite spirit.

Joy is that "ah-ha" moment when you know that you know that everything is going to be alright.

Joy is welcomed in every season, be it fall, winter, spring, or summer. It is welcomed during the season of a fruitful harvest and even during the season of an extreme severe famine. So when Joy shows up, do not disregard.

Joy is too valuable to hold onto. It becomes even more priceless when you share it.

For every problem there's a solution.
It's Joy!

Joy is a gift that doesn't need wrapping.

You radiate Joy when you let the
Son shine in.

The garment of Joy is always fashionable.

Thanksgiving is the launching pad
for Joy.

Joy is Jesus looking at you and calling you His beloved.

Joy is giving someone a warm friendly smile and a "High-five".

Joy is having grace for the race.

Joy and Thanksgiving really do make a great team.

Joy never tires or retires.

Happiness may flee but not
Joy; It lingers.

Jesus came, lived, suffered, died,
rose again and lives today so
that we might have everlasting Joy
here on earth and eternal Joy in Heaven.

Joy! There's always an opportunity for it.

Joy is the remote control that changes your attitude. Use it often. You will get great reception.

Joy and Praise enjoy each other's company.

Joy is not an experiment; It's an experience.

Joy is letting go of all of those issues and issuing them to God.

CPSIA information can be obtained
at www.ICGtesting.com
Printed in the USA
BVHW040104151221
624021BV00015B/2009